R. Euphrates

GREAT SEA

Sea of Galilee

GALILEE

Nazareth

CAESAREA

SAMARIA

DECAPOLIS

R. Jordan

R. Euphrates

Nineveh

R. Tigris

Jericho

JERUSALEM

PERAEA

JUDEA

Bethlehem

Gaza

DEAD SEA

BABYLONIA

Beer-Sheba

Baghdad

IDUMAEA

THE HOLY LAND
in the time of JESUS

Desert

Babylon

LANDS
OF THE
BIBLE

CHALDEA

Ur

PERSIAN GULF

MILES

0   100   200   300

Series 649

The Bible has many references to animals, birds, trees and flowers, and this fascinating book illustrates in full colour those most frequently mentioned. It also describes the part they played in the lives of the people of the Old and New Testaments.

Animals, Birds and Plants of the Bible

by HILDA I. ROSTRON
with illustrations by
CLIVE UPTTON

Publishers: Ladybird Books Ltd . Loughborough
© Ladybird Books Ltd (formerly Wills & Hepworth Ltd) 1964
Printed in England

SHEEP

In Bible times a man was regarded as rich if he possessed many sheep, goats and cattle.

Genesis c.13 vv.2,3

Abraham was a rich man. He and his family lived in tents so that they could be constantly moving in search of new pastures for their flocks. These animals provided the family with all they needed to live. Sheep were a source of milk and meat, and their wool was used for making clothes.

Psalm 23

There are many accounts of shepherds and sheep in the Bible. One of the best known is in Psalm 23, said to have been written by David the shepherd boy, who later became King David.

The shepherd did not drive his sheep; he led them. He wore a sheep-skin cloak, and carried a short wooden rod as a weapon against wild animals. He also had a long staff or crook, and a sling. The sling was used for aiming stones to check any sheep from straying.

7214 0188 0

GOATS

The domestic goat can still be seen in herds in Bible lands, and is often looked after by the same shepherd who cares for the sheep. Goats are very hardy animals, and manage to find enough to eat even where grass is scarce.

Exodus c.26 v.7
In Bible times, strong light tents were woven from goat-hair. This was also woven into cloth for garments, curtains or other useful things. We read of eleven large curtains being woven from goat-hair, and made into a tent over the Tabernacle.

Luke c.15 v.29
These animals were a source of meat, and butter and cheese were made from their milk. The meat of the kid was eaten as a special dish at feasts when 'making merry' or entertaining friends. Bottles to hold water, wine, milk or other fluids were made from goat-skin.

Even the poorest family possessed at least one goat.

1 Samuel c.24 vv.1,2
Wild goats live in rocky places, and are very shy. 'En-gedi' is a place-name meaning 'The Fountain of the Wild Goat or Kid'.

THE ASS

The domestic ass is often mentioned in the Bible. It was, and still is, an important animal in the life of the people of Palestine.

This ass was larger than the animal we know, and could probably work harder and longer. It was used for riding, for carrying burdens, and for turning heavy millstones. When pulling a plough, the ass was often yoked to an ox or oxen.

Job c.1 v.3

The Bible states that Job was the greatest of all men of the East. Part of his wealth was the possession of five hundred she asses. Abraham was a rich man and rode upon an ass, travelling from Beersheba to Mount Moriah.

Genesis c.22 v.3

Judges c.5 v.10

The colour of the ass is usually drab, but there are white ones. When we read, 'ye that ride on white asses', this refers to noblemen, who greatly valued these animals. Owning white asses was a sign of wealth.

Job c.39 vv.5,8

In Bible times wild asses roamed the countryside searching for pasture and water.

Matthew c.21 vv.2,5,7

The Lord Jesus rode into Jerusalem upon a young ass, 'a colt, the foal of an ass'. Palm Sunday is the day when this ride is celebrated.

THE CAMEL

In desert lands the camel is a most valued animal, and was so in Bible times. It can carry heavy burdens, and cover as much as thirty miles a day with a load of nearly half a ton. It can also last a long while without food or water.

The hair from the camel was woven into cloth, and used for tent making and for saddle bags.

Matthew c.3 v.4

John the Baptist wore a prophet's dress woven from camel's hair. His leather belt was probably made from camel-skin. This was also used for the making of war shields, for harness, saddle bags, bottles and sandals.

Genesis c.31 v.34

A camel's furniture included a big wooden frame which fitted over the hump. Rachel hid images inside such furniture. The framework was covered with a brightly coloured cloth or carpet when the camel was saddled.

1 Samuel c.30 v.17

In a battle which David fought and won, 'four hundred young men who rode camels' escaped with their lives.

THE HORSE

Joshua
c.17 v.16
In early Bible times the ass was the main means of transport used by the Hebrews. When we read of horses, the reference is usually to war horses. The early Hebrews were said not to own horses, though the Canaanites had horses and chariots of war.

2 Samuel
c.8 v.4
Later, King David kept some of the chariots and horses captured in battle. When the Israelites returned from exile, they brought with them six thousand seven hundred and twenty asses, and only seven hundred and thirty-six horses.

Ezra
c.2 v.66

1 Kings
c.4 v.26
King Solomon equipped his army with many chariots for which he needed horses. Apparently he also traded in them, obtaining horses from Egypt and selling them to his northern neighbours.

Job
c.39 vv.19-25
The Assyrians were proud of their horses. They decorated the harness with bells and designs of metal attached to the leather. There is a fine description of a war horse in the Book of Job.

THE CONEY OR HYRAX

Proverbs c.30 v.26
This animal is described as one of four little things 'exceeding wise', because though it was of a 'feeble folk' it was clever enough to make its home in the rocks as a protection against other animals.

Psalm 104 v.18
Though 'coney' is translated as 'rabbit', it is not a rabbit but a Rock Badger or Hyrax. It is about the same size and colour as the rabbit, and is quick in running to its rocky hiding place at the least sign of danger. Its ears are round, not long. Unlike the rabbit, it does not burrow into the ground. The hyrax lives with others in a colony, and its food is grassy reeds and any vegetables it can find.

Often these creatures can be seen basking in the sunshine, but they are always alert and cautious, and never move far from their homes. Some always act as sentinels to warn of danger.

The Hebrew name for the coney or hyrax is 'shapen' — meaning 'one who hides'.

THE JACKAL

In the Holy Land, on the edge of the desert places, there are large numbers of rocks and caves which in Bible times provided dens and hiding places for the jackal. These animals prowled about in packs, looking for stray sheep, lambs or kids, and for small animals and birds.

Jeremiah c.9 v.11

Bible passages which describe desolate places include jackals as being among the wild creatures wandering there.

Isaiah c.34 v.13

One earlier Bible version uses the word 'dragon' in some references. This is now understood to mean 'jackal'.

Jeremiah c.14 v.6

Jeremiah paints a word picture of wild asses snuffling through wide nostrils like (dragons) jackals, trying to scent out grass, of which there was none. Later we read of ruined Babylon being a dwelling place for these animals. We can well imagine the desolate sound of their howling.

The common jackal of Palestine has a tawny, yellowish coat.

THE LION

The lion has been mentioned in the Bible more times than any other wild beast, and there are many references to its roaring, its appetite and its den. For many years it has not been seen in Palestine.

Judges c.14 vv.5,6

Samson killed a young lion that was prowling in a vineyard. David told King Saul how he caught and killed a lion that stole a lamb from the flock. One way of capturing lions was to dig a pit into which they fell. A man who had done mighty deeds went down a pit on a snowy day and killed a lion.

1 Samuel c.17 v.36

2 Samuel c.23 v.20

Job c.4 v.11

The natural death of a lion is referred to —the time when it grows too old to catch its prey, and dies of hunger.

Daniel c.6

Perhaps the best-known Bible story about lions is that of Daniel being cast into a lions' den—and of God protecting him from harm.

THE DOVE

We read about the dove many times in the Bible, and more than any other bird.

Genesis c.8 v.8

Three times Noah sent a dove from the Ark. The first time it returned 'finding no rest for the sole of her foot'. The flood waters were still high. The second time she returned with an olive leaf in her beak: this meant that the tree tops were to be seen. The third time the dove did not return: at last a place to rest and nest had been found.

Song of Solomon c.2 v.12

We read that 'the time of the singing of birds is come, and the voice of the turtle (dove) is heard'. This refers to the return of the turtle dove from the south where it had wintered. The sound of its voice meant that Spring had really come.

Isaiah c.38 v.14

The dove's song sounds very sad; so when we read 'I did mourn as a dove', we can easily understand how the writer felt.

Matthew c.21 v.12

Matthew tells us that when Jesus was in the Temple, he overthrew the tables of those who sold doves.

Matthew c.3 v.16

We remember the dove especially as the emblem of the Holy Spirit. When Jesus was baptized by John the Baptist, the Holy Spirit descended in the form of a dove.

THE EAGLE

Jeremiah
c.49 v.16
The eagle is frequently mentioned in the Bible. Its nobility and grandeur, great strength and swiftness of flight, its nesting place, are all referred to with such words as

Job
c.39 vv.27-30
. . . 'Make thy nest as high as the eagle'; 'His horses are swifter than eagles'. 'Though thy nest be set among the stars,' poetically

Obadiah v.4
describes the place of the eagle's nest on the top of a high crag. Here the young ones were kept safely while the parent birds

Isaiah
c.40 v.31
circled the hills and valleys seeking food.

The eagle's beak shows it to be a flesh-eating bird. The feet, with long toes and sharp talons, easily grasps and holds its prey, enabling it to carry off young lambs.

The Hebrew word for 'eagle' also refers to certain vultures, and translations sometimes vary. Matthew, chapter 24, verse 28, probably refers to vultures—not eagles.

THE RAVEN

*Genesis
c.8 v.7*

The raven is the first bird mentioned by name in the Bible. Noah doubtless chose this bird to scan the flood waters because of its size and strength, being able to fly far and wide, and—because it is a scavenger—being able to feed on the dead bodies of any birds or animals floating on the water. We read that it flew 'to and fro until the waters were abated (dried up)'.

*1 Kings
c.17 vv.4,6*

We can also read of ravens bringing food to the prophet Elijah at brook Cherith. Ravens no doubt visited this place because of the water, trees, rocks, and the abundance of small birds and wild creatures on which they could feed. The Bible says that the ravens brought Elijah bread and meat, morning and evening, but just exactly what kind of food this was is uncertain.

*Luke
c.12 v.24*

When Jesus was telling his disciples that God would take care of their needs, he pointed out that God cared even for the ravens and fed them too.

THE STORK

Jeremiah c.8 v.7
A Bible verse reads: '. . . the stork in the heavens knoweth her appointed times'. These words refer to the regular arrival of storks in Palestine at about the end of March. They probably came from Africa. Usually appearing in the daytime, these large, wide-winged birds were quickly noticed and welcomed by the people, who were glad of this sign of Spring.

The storks would settle by lakes, marshes and rivers and start fishing for food. Fish, frogs, lizards, small reptiles and large insects would be hungrily sought by the newly arrived migrants.

Psalm 104 v.17
It is possible that David, the lover of nature, was a bird-watcher. He describes the nesting of the stork in the tall fir trees of Lebanon: '. . . as for the stork, the fir trees are her house'. The flat branches of the fir would provide a good foundation for the nests.

It is said that the Hebrew word for 'stork' means pious and kind, which shows that the stork's kindness to its young, and its dutifulness, had been noted.

Leviticus c.11 v.19
It was forbidden to eat the flesh of the stork.

THE OSTRICH

In the Bible, this tall bird is particularly associated with wild and desert places. Its natural food is vegetable, but under wild conditions it will eat anything that can be eaten; snakes, lizards, birds and insects.

Job c.39 vv.13-19 Its legs are long and muscular, and it is said to be able to travel at sixty miles an hour. A reference to its. speed says—'it laughs at the horse and its rider'. The ostrich has only two toes, and these are armed with short, blunt nails. Legs, feet and strong beak are used as weapons of attack.

This chapter also refers to the fact that the ostrich neglects her eggs, and is indifferent to her young—'as though they were not hers'.

An ostrich egg weighs about three pounds, and the fluffy chicks are grey-brown—the size of a domestic hen.

SWALLOWS AND SWIFTS

Psalm 84 v.3 We read in one of the Psalms of the swallow finding 'a nest where she may lay her young: even thy altars, O Lord of Hosts'.

Jeremiah c.8 v.7 The Bible refers to the annual migration of these birds—'they observed the time of their coming'.

In the warm climate of the Holy Land, the glassless windows and stone lattices gave easy entry for birds, which built their nests inside the walls, the roofs and rafters of the houses, as well as in the Temple itself.

Isaiah c.38 v.14 Birds which made their homes in sacred buildings were kept unharmed. The 'chatter' referred to in Isaiah, was their ceaseless twittering.

Insect pests abounding in the hot weather were caught by parent birds to feed themselves and their young. Probably the villagers welcomed the ceaseless hunt of the birds after harmful garden pests.

THE FIG TREE

In a hot country like Palestine, any tree which gives shade is welcome. The fig tree, which can grow to a height of over thirty feet, is valued for its leafy foliage as well as for its fruit—which it bears for ten months of the year.

1 Kings c.4 v.25 In the First Book of Kings we read that 'every man dwelt safely under his own vine and under his own fig tree.'

1 Samuel c.30 v.12 The fruit was eaten fresh, or dried and pressed together into cakes to store for winter. King David gave a piece of fig cake to an exhausted Egyptian soldier fallen in battle. The man must have been glad of the fruit, as he had not eaten for three days.

1 Samuel c.25 v.18 Two hundred cakes of figs were part of a peace offering which David had given to him for his men by Abigail. The gift was so big that it was carried on the backs of asses.

2 Kings c.20 v.7 Figs were used for medicinal purposes also, and Hezekiah was cured of a boil by the application of a poultice of figs.

THE VINE

Isaiah
c.5 vv.2,5

We read about the vine and the vine-yards many times in the Bible. The grape-bearing vine was of great value to the people of Palestine. Vines were trained to grow over trellis or posts, over walls and in courtyards. They were often planted near fig trees, in whose branches they entwined naturally.

Psalm 80
vv. 8-12

Mark
c.12 v.1

If the vineyard was big, a hedge or wall surrounded it for protection. Keepers of the vineyard kept a look-out against prowling animals which might spoil the vines. The look-out men had rough stone huts or 'towers' roofed with earth.

Isaiah
c.16 v.10

Leviticus
c.19 v.10

The harvesting of grapes was a time of special thanksgiving. When the vineyard owner had harvested the grapes, the left-over fruit was gathered by the poor. The grapes were tipped into a vat, and the juice trodden out with bare feet. Treading out of grapes was accompanied by joyful shouting and singing.

Isaiah
c.63 vv.2,3

Jeremiah
c.48 v.33

Though mainly used for making wine, the grapes were sometimes eaten fresh, and also dried for food as raisins.

THE DATE-PALM TREE

Jeremiah c.10 v.5

The fruit of the date-palm tree was, and still is, a familiar food in Palestine. The Bible refers to the palm tree's grace and beauty, its height, its colour and its fruitfulness even in its old age. But there seems to be no definite reference to the fruit.

Psalm 92 vv.12-14

Palm trees grew at Elim where the Israelites camped after crossing the Red Sea. There was an oasis of twelve springs around which seventy palm trees grew.

Deuteronomy c.34 v.3

In ancient times, Jericho was known as the city of palm trees. Branches or leaves of the palm were used to make out-door huts or booths for the Feast of the Tabernacles. The people camped in these booths during the week of festivities, celebrating the harvesting of corn and fruit.

Leviticus c.23 v.40

The palm tree and basket of dates were stamped on coins in early times. Palm trees were to be seen in the carvings decorating Solomon's temple.

John c.12 v.13

The Lord Jesus was greeted with waving palm branches on his ride into Jerusalem.

THE OLIVE TREE

Genesis c.8 v.11
The olive is the first tree we read about in the Bible. It was an olive leaf which the dove brought to Noah in the Ark.

Olive trees grow to a great age. Some olive trees are shrub-like; others grow to about twenty or thirty feet high, and as much as six gallons of olive oil can be obtained from their fruit every two years.

Deuteronomy c.24 v.20
After the fruit is harvested, the berries are pressed to extract the oil. We read of olives being pressed, or trodden by the feet.
Exodus c.27 v.20
In Bible times, as now, olive oil was of considerable value. It was used as food, for cooking, as fuel for oil lamps, as a healing medicine and for soothing and cleansing the
Luke c.10 v.34
skin.

1 Samuel c.16 v.13
Olive oil was used at times of special ceremony. The man chosen to be king or priest had his head anointed with oil.

1 Kings c.6 vv.31,32
The doors and posts of Solomon's Temple were made of olive wood, and the figures of cherubim in the sanctuary were also carved from olive wood.

THE CEDAR TREE

2 Kings
c.19 v.23

Isaiah
c.14 v.8
c.37 v.24

Though to-day there are no more than a group of about four hundred of these magnificent trees, the cedars of Lebanon were once famous all over the ancient world.

2 Samuel
c.5 v.11

This tree can grow to a height of more than one hundred feet. It has long branches which spread horizontally, and its straight grained, sweet-smelling wood was much sought after by kings for building their palaces, temples and ships, and for furniture and interior panelling. King David fitted out his palace with this wood, and King Solomon used it when building his palace and his famous temple.

1 Chronicles
c.14 v.1

1 Kings
c.6 & 7

2 Kings
c.14 v.9

Reference to the cedar is made many times in the Bible, in which it is frequently mentioned as the symbol of power and beauty. Because it was always green and strong, it was likened to the righteous who always had a strong and constant faith in God.

Isaiah
c.41 v.19

Isaiah prophesied the day when God would change the desert and plant cedars and other great trees.

40

FLOWERS OF THE FIELD

Matthew c.6 v.28

In April, Palestine has carpets of brilliant flowers growing in the fields. The flowers that catch the eye are the multi-coloured anemones: scarlet, white, purple and blue. They grow on the lower hills, by the wayside and in the fields.

It is thought by some students of the Bible that 'lily' was used to include flowers in general: the rose, iris, gladiolus, narcissus, jasmine and anemone being only some of the beautiful flowers familiar to our Lord. He believed the glory of the 'lily' to be greater than the royal robes of King Solomon.

Psalm 103 vv.15,16

The wind and the hot sun soon shortens the life of the flowers. We read of the grass of the field, including withered flowers, being cast into the oven as fuel. This refers to the brick oven of the old days, when dried grass, brushwood and brambles were used for fuel. We also read of thorns crackling under the cooking pot.

Matthew c.6 v.30

Ecclesiastes c.7 v.6

THE FLAX PLANT

Exodus c.9 v.31
Flax was an important plant grown in early times. The prepared fibre was spun to make linen and various articles, and is often mentioned in the Bible.

Joshua c.2 v.6
After the crop was pulled, it was spread on the flat roof of the house to dry. We read of Rahab hiding the spies among the stalks of flax.

Isaiah c.19 v.9
When the flax had dried, it was combed, or heckled, to separate the outer layer from the fibre underneath. A busy housewife is described as seeking wool and flax, and *Proverbs c.31 vv.13,19,22* working with her hands: that is, weaving cloth and making linen garments.

Exodus c.28
The finest linen was worn by the Jewish priests, and the curtains of the Tabernacle were also embroidered upon the same *Exodus c.26 v.1* material.

Sails, measuring lines and ropes were made from flax, and one use of the coarse part, or tow, was for lamp wicks.

HERBS

Deuteronomy
c.14 v.22

In Bible times, herbs were used in the preparation of food and as medicine. Tithes and taxes were paid on many things in the time of our Lord, including some herbs. He rebuked the Pharisees for being more concerned about the payment of tithes 'for mint and rue and all manner of herbs' than about the true worship of God.

Luke
c.11 v.42

Isaiah
c.28 v.25

Palestine mint was not unlike our garden mint. Anise, or dill, was used as a medicine and for flavouring. The cummin plant was 'beaten with a rod' to release the ripe seeds, which looked like caraway seeds. Rue was used as a medicine and as a spice.

Luke
c.13 v.19

Mustard was 'the greatest among herbs'. Jesus noted the smallness of its seed, and compared its growth to the Kingdom of Heaven. A plant or tree, about ten feet high and big enough to house nesting birds, can grow from this tiny seed.

Exodus
c.12 v.8

Bitter herbs had to be eaten with the meat at the Feast of the Passover; this was to remind those who ate them of the bitterness of enslavement to the Egyptians.

REEDS AND RUSHES

Exodus
c.2 v.3
The cradle basket-boat made to hide the baby Moses from King Pharoah was woven from bulrushes. The tough stalks were pliable, and could be twisted into mats and baskets. We read of boats, or skiffs, being made from rushes, and even
Isaiah
c.18 v.2
to-day some are still made.

Another name for this very tall plant was 'papyrus'. We get our word 'paper' from this plant's name. In Bible times the pith inside the strong branches of this reed was carefully peeled and flattened. The thin strips were pasted side-by-side and across each other, then hammered and pressed. The papyrus was dried, and the surface rubbed smooth ready for writing.

Jeremiah
c.36 v.2
Lengths of papyrus were glued end-to-end for lengthy written work. This, when finished, was rolled up. We read in the Old Testament of a Roll of a Book. This would probably be made of papyrus.

Ezekiel
c.40 vv.3,5
Revelations
c.21 v.15
Small thin reeds were cut to make pens, and longer reeds were used as measuring rods.

BIBLE GARDENS

Because of the difficulties of irrigation, gardens were not usual in Palestine, and those of the Hebrews seem mainly to have been of trees, to give shade and fruit, and of sweetly scented plants and herbs rather than solely of flowers.

Some beautiful gardens are described in The Song of Songs, but there are few other mentions in the Old Testament.

1 Kings c.21 v.2 Herb gardens were greatly valued, and King Ahab asked Naboth to give him his vineyard so that a herb garden could be made out of it.

John c.19 v.41 The Garden of Gethsemane, where the Lord Jesus went to pray, was undoubtedly planted with olive trees, as the name means 'the place of the oil press'.

Gardens were used as burying places, and we can read of Pilate giving permission for the body of Jesus to be buried in a garden belonging to Joseph of Arimethea.

Ecclesiastes c.2 vv.5,6
Isaiah c.58 v.11
A good supply of water was a special need for gardens in the hot, dry climate of Palestine. This was usually drawn from a fountain, spring or well nearby.